The Right Honourable

SIR WINSTON CHURCHILL

K.G., O.M., C.H., M.P.

PAINTING

AS A

PASTIME

CORNERSTONE LIBRARY
NEW YORK

The hardcover edition of this book was published in the United States in 1950 by The McGraw-Hill Book Company, Inc. This new Cornerstone Library edition is a complete and unabridged reprint of that original hardcover publication, and is published by arrangement with Odhams Press Ltd., of London, England.

Reprinted 1965

The essay "Painting as a Pastime" is reprinted from Sir Winston Churchill's book Amid These Storms *(copyright, 1932) by permission of the publishers, Charles Scribner's Sons, N. Y.*

CORNERSTONE LIBRARY PUBLICATIONS
Are Distributed By
Affiliated Publishers
A Division of Pocket Books, Inc.
Rockefeller Center
630 Fifth Avenue, New York 20, N.Y.

Manufactured in the United States of America
under the supervision of
Rolls Offset Printing Co., Inc., N.Y.

Contents

v

Painting as a Pastime

MANY remedies are suggested for the avoidance of worry and mental overstrain by persons who, over prolonged periods, have to bear exceptional responsibilities and discharge duties upon a very large scale. Some advise exercise, and others, repose. Some counsel travel, and others, retreat. Some praise solitude, and others, gaiety. No doubt all these may play their part according to the individual temperament. But the element which is constant and common in all of them is Change.

Change is the master key. A man can wear out a particular part of his mind by continually using it and tiring it, just in the same way as he can wear out the elbows of his coat. There is, however, this difference between the living cells of the brain and inanimate articles: one cannot mend the frayed elbows of a coat by rubbing the sleeves or shoulders; but the tired parts of the mind can be rested and strengthened, not merely by rest, but by using other parts. It is not enough merely to switch off the lights which play upon the main and ordinary field of interest; a new field of interest must be illuminated. It is no use saying to the tired 'mental muscles'—if one may coin such an expression —'I will give you a good rest,' 'I will go for a long walk,' or 'I will lie down and think of nothing.' The mind keeps busy just the same. If it has been weighing and measuring, it goes on weighing and measuring. If it has been worrying, it goes on worrying. It is only when new cells are called into activity, when new stars become the lords of the ascendant, that relief, repose, refreshment are afforded.

A gifted American psychologist has said, 'Worry is a spasm of the emotion; the mind catches hold of something and will not let it go.' It is useless to argue with the mind in this condition. The stronger the will, the more futile the task. One can only gently insinuate something else into its convulsive grasp. And if this something else is rightly chosen, if it is really attended by the illumination of another field of interest, gradually, and often quite swiftly, the old undue grip relaxes and the process of recuperation and repair begins.

The cultivation of a hobby and new forms of interest is therefore a policy of first importance to a public man. But this is not a business that can be undertaken in a day or swiftly improvised by a mere command of the will. The growth of alternative mental interests is a long process. The seeds must be carefully chosen; they must fall on good ground; they must be sedulously tended, if the vivifying fruits are to be at hand when needed.

To be really happy and really safe, one ought to have at least two or three hobbies, and they must all be real. It is no use starting late in life to say: 'I will take an interest in this or that.' Such an attempt only aggravates the strain of mental effort. A man may acquire great knowledge of topics unconnected with his daily work, and yet hardly get any benefit or relief. It is no use doing what you like; you have got to like what you do. Broadly speaking, human beings may be divided into three classes: those who are toiled to death, those who are worried to death, and those who are bored to death. It is no use offering the manual labourer, tired out with a hard week's sweat and effort, the chance of playing a game of football or baseball on Saturday afternoon. It is no use inviting the politician or the professional or business man, who has been working or worrying about serious things for six days, to work or worry about trifling things at the week-end.

As for the unfortunate people who can command everything they want, who can gratify every caprice and lay their hands on almost every object of desire—for them a new pleasure, a new excitement is only an additional satiation. In vain they rush frantically round from place to place, trying to escape from avenging boredom by mere clatter and motion. For them discipline in one form or another is the most hopeful path.

It may also be said that rational, industrious, useful human beings are divided into two classes: first, those whose work is work and whose pleasure is pleasure; and secondly, those whose work and pleasure are one. Of these the former are the majority. They have their compensations. The long hours in the office or the factory bring with them as their reward, not only the means of sustenance, but a keen appetite for pleasure even in its simplest and most modest forms. But Fortune's favoured children belong to the second class. Their life is a natural harmony. For them the working hours are never long enough. Each day is a holiday, and ordinary holidays when they come are grudged as enforced interruptions in an absorbing vocation. Yet to both classes the need of an alternative outlook, of a change of atmosphere, of a diversion of effort, is essential. Indeed, it may well be that those whose work is their pleasure are those who most need the means of banishing it at intervals from their minds.

The most common form of diversion is reading. In that vast and varied field millions find their mental comfort. Nothing makes a man more reverent than a library. 'A few books,' which was Lord Morley's definition of anything under five thousand, may give a sense of comfort and even of complacency. But a day in a library, even of modest dimensions, quickly dispels these illusory sensations. As you browse about, taking down book after book from the shelves and contemplating the vast, infinitely varied store of knowledge and wisdom which the human race has accumulated and preserved, pride, even in its most innocent forms, is chased from the heart by feelings of awe not untinged with sadness. As one surveys the mighty array of sages, saints, historians, scientists, poets and philosophers whose treasures one will never be able to admire—still less enjoy—the brief tenure of our existence here dominates mind and spirit.

Think of all the wonderful tales that have been told, and well told, which you will never know. Think of all the searching inquiries into matters of great consequence which you will never pursue. Think of all the delighting or disturbing ideas that you will never share. Think of the mighty labours which have been accomplished for your service, but of which you will never reap the harvest. But from this melancholy there also comes a calm. The bitter sweets of a pious despair melt into an agreeable sense of compulsory resignation from which we turn with renewed zest to the lighter vanities of life.

'What shall I do with all my books?' was the question; and the answer, 'Read them,' sobered the questioner. But if you cannot read them, at any rate handle them and, as it were, fondle them. Peer into them. Let them fall open where they will. Read on from the first sentence that arrests the eye. Then turn to another. Make a voyage of discovery, taking soundings of uncharted seas. Set them back on their shelves with your own hands. Arrange them on your own plan, so that if you do not know what is in them, you at least know where they are. If they cannot be your friends, let them at any rate be your acquaintances. If they cannot enter the circle of your life, do not deny them at least a nod of recognition.

It is a mistake to read too many good books when quite young. A man once told me that he had read all the books that mattered. Cross-questioned, he appeared to have read a great many, but they seemed to have made only a slight impression. How many had he understood? How many had entered into his mental composition? How many had been hammered on the anvils of his mind, and afterwards ranged in an armoury of bright weapons ready to hand?

It is a great pity to read a book too soon in life. The first impression is the one that counts; and if it is a slight one, it may be all that can be hoped for. A later and second perusal may recoil from a surface already hardened by premature contact. Young people should be careful in their reading, as old people in eating their food. They should not eat too much. They should chew it well.

Since change is an essential element in diversion of all kinds, it is naturally more restful and refreshing to read in a different language from that in which one's ordinary daily work is done. To have a second language at your disposal, even if you only know it enough to read it with pleasure, is a sensible advantage. Our educationists are too often anxious to teach children so many different languages that they never get far enough in any one to derive any use or enjoyment from their study. The boy learns enough Latin to detest it; enough Greek to pass an examination; enough French to get from Calais to Paris; enough German to exhibit a diploma; enough Spanish or Italian to tell which is which; but not enough of any to secure the enormous boon of access to a second literature. Choose well, choose wisely, and choose one. Concentrate upon that one. Do not be content until you find yourself reading in it with real enjoyment. The process of reading for pleasure in another language rests the mental muscles; it enlivens the mind by a different sequence and emphasis of ideas. The mere form of speech excites the activity of separate brain-cells, relieving in the most effective manner the fatigue of those in hackneyed use. One may imagine that a man who blew the trumpet for his living would be glad to play the violin for his amusement. So it is with reading in another language than your own.

But reading and book-love in all their forms suffer from one serious defect: they are too nearly akin to the ordinary daily round of the brain-worker to give that element of change and contrast essential to real relief. To restore psychic equilibrium we should call into use those parts of the mind which direct both eye and hand. Many men have found great advantage in practising a handicraft for pleasure. Joinery, chemistry, book-binding, even brick-laying—if one were interested in them and skilful at them —would give a real relief to the over-tired brain. But, best of all and easiest to procure are sketching and painting in all their forms. I consider myself very lucky that late in life I have been able to develop this new taste and pastime. Painting came to my rescue in a most trying time, and I shall venture in the pages that follow to express the gratitude I feel.

Painting is a companion with whom one may hope to walk a great part of life's journey,

> '*Age cannot wither her nor custom stale*
> *Her infinite variety.*'

One by one the more vigorous sports and exacting games fall away. Exceptional exertions are purchased only by a more pronounced and more prolonged fatigue. Muscles may relax, and feet and hands slow down; the nerve of youth and manhood may become less trusty. But painting is a friend who makes no undue demands, excites to no exhausting pursuits, keeps faithful pace even with feeble steps, and holds her canvas as a screen between us and the envious eyes of Time or the surly advance of Decrepitude.

Happy are the painters, for they shall not be lonely. Light and colour, peace and hope, will keep them company to the end, or almost to the end, of the day.

13

To have reached the age of forty without ever handling a brush or fiddling with a pencil, to have regarded with mature eye the painting of pictures of any kind as a mystery, to have stood agape before the chalk of the pavement artist, and then suddenly to find oneself plunged in the middle of a new and intense form of interest and action with paints and palettes and canvases, and not to be discouraged by results, is an astonishing and enriching experience. I hope it may be shared by others. I should be glad if these lines induced others to try the experiment which I have tried, and if some at least were to find themselves dowered with an absorbing new amusement delightful to themselves, and at any rate not violently harmful to man or beast.

I hope this is modest enough: because there is no subject on which I feel more humble or yet at the same time more natural. I do not presume to explain how to paint, but only how to get enjoyment. Do not turn the superior eye of critical passivity upon these efforts. Buy a paint-box and have a try. If you need something to occupy your leisure, to divert your mind from the daily round, to illuminate your holidays, do not be too ready to believe that you cannot find what you want here. Even at the advanced age of forty! It would be a sad pity to shuffle or scramble along through one's playtime with golf and bridge, pottering, loitering, shifting from one heel to the other, wondering what on earth to do—as perhaps is the fate of some unhappy beings—when all the while, if you only knew, there is close at hand a wonderful new world of thought and craft, a sunlit garden gleaming with light and colour of which you have the key in your waistcoat-pocket. Inexpensive independence, a mobile and perennial pleasure apparatus, new mental food and exercise, the old harmonies and symmetries in an entirely different language, an added interest to every common scene, an occupation for every idle hour, an unceasing voyage of entrancing discovery—these are high prizes. Make quite sure they are not yours. After all, if you try, and fail, there is not much harm done. The nursery will grab what the studio has rejected. And then you can always go out and kill some animal, humiliate some rival on the links, or despoil some friend across the green table. You will not be worse off in any way. In fact you will be better off. You will know 'beyond a peradventure,' to quote a phrase disagreeably reminiscent, that that is really what you were meant to do in your hours of relaxation.

But if, on the contrary, you are inclined—late in life though it be—to reconnoitre a foreign sphere of limitless extent, then be persuaded that the first quality that is needed is Audacity. There really is no time for the deliberate approach. Two years of drawing-lessons, three years of copying woodcuts, five years of plaster casts—these are for the young. They have enough to bear. And this thorough grounding is for those who, hearing the call in the morning of their days, are able to make painting their paramount lifelong vocation. The truth and beauty of line and form which by the slightest touch or twist of the brush a real artist imparts to every feature of his design must be founded on long, hard, persevering apprenticeship and a practice so habitual that it has become instinctive. We must not be too ambitious. We cannot aspire to masterpieces. We may content ourselves with a joy ride in a paint-box. And for this Audacity is the only ticket.

I shall now relate my personal experience. When I left the Admiralty at the end of May, 1915, I still remained a member of the Cabinet and of the War Council. In this position I knew everything and could do nothing. The change from the intense executive activities of each day's work at the Admiralty to the narrowly measured duties of a counsellor left me gasping. Like a sea-beast fished up from the depths, or a diver too suddenly hoisted, my veins threatened to burst from the fall in pressure. I had great anxiety and no means of relieving it; I had vehement convictions and small power to give effect to them. I had to watch the unhappy casting-away of great opportunities, and the feeble execution of plans which I had launched and in which I heartily believed. I had long hours of utterly unwonted leisure in which to contemplate the frightful unfolding of the War. At a moment when every fibre of my being was inflamed to action, I was forced to remain a spectator of the tragedy, placed cruelly in a front seat. And then it was that the Muse of Painting came to my rescue—out of charity and out of chivalry, because after all she had nothing to do with me—and said, 'Are these toys any good to you? They amuse some people.'

Some experiments one Sunday in the country with the children's paint-box led me to procure the next morning a complete outfit for painting in oils.

Having bought the colours, an easel, and a canvas, the next step was *to begin*. But what a step to take! The palette gleamed with beads of colour; fair and white rose the canvas; the empty brush hung poised, heavy with destiny, irresolute in the air. My hand seemed arrested by a silent veto. But after all the sky on this occasion was unquestionably blue, and a pale blue at that. There could be no doubt that blue paint mixed with white should be put on the top part of the canvas. One really does not need to have had an artist's training to see that. It is a starting-point open to all. So very gingerly I mixed a little blue paint on the palette with a very small brush, and then with infinite precaution made a mark about as big as a bean upon the affronted snow-white shield. It was a challenge, a deliberate challenge; but so subdued, so halting, indeed so cataleptic, that it deserved no response. At that moment the loud approaching sound of a motor-car was heard in the drive. From this chariot there stepped swiftly and lightly none other than the gifted wife of Sir John Lavery. 'Painting! But what are you hesitating about? Let me have a brush—the big one.' Splash into the turpentine, wallop into the blue and the white, frantic flourish on the palette—clean no longer—and then several large, fierce strokes and slashes of blue on the absolutely cowering canvas. Anyone could see that it could not hit back. No evil fate avenged the jaunty violence. The canvas grinned in helplessness before me. The spell was broken. The sickly inhibitions rolled away. I seized the largest brush and fell upon my victim with Berserk fury. I have never felt any awe of a canvas since.

Everyone knows the feelings with which one stands shivering on a spring-board, the shock when a friendly foe steals up behind and hurls you into the flood, and the ardent glow which thrills you as you emerge breathless from the plunge.

This beginning with Audacity, or being thrown into the middle of it, is already a very great part of the art of painting. But there is more in it than that.

> *'La peinture à l'huile*
> *Est bien difficile,*
> *Mais c'est beaucoup plus beau*
> *Que la peinture à l'eau.'*

I write no word in disparagement of water-colours. But there really is nothing like oils. You have a medium at your disposal which offers real power, if you only can find out how to use it. Moreover, it is easier to get a certain distance along the road by its means than by water-colour. First of all, you can correct mistakes much more easily. One sweep of the palette-knife 'lifts' the blood and tears of a morning from the canvas and enables a fresh start to be made; indeed the canvas is all the better for past impressions. Secondly, you can approach your problem from any direction. You need not build downwards awkwardly from white paper to your darkest dark. You may strike where you please, beginning if you will with a moderate central arrangement of middle tones, and then hurling in the extremes when the psychological moment comes. Lastly, the pigment itself is such nice stuff to handle (if it does not retaliate). You can build it on layer after layer

18

if you like. You can keep on experimenting. You can change your plan to meet the exigencies of time or weather. And always remember you can scrape it all away.

Just to paint is great fun. The colours are lovely to look at and delicious to squeeze out. Matching them, however crudely, with what you see is fascinating and absolutely absorbing. Try it if you have not done so—before you die. As one slowly begins to escape from the difficulties of choosing the right colours and laying them on in the right places and in the right way, wider considerations come into view. One begins to see, for instance, that painting a picture is like fighting a battle; and trying to paint a picture is, I suppose, like trying to fight a battle. It is, if anything, more exciting than fighting it successfully. But the principle is the same. It is the same kind of problem as unfolding a long, sustained, interlocked argument. It is a proposition which, whether of few or numberless parts, is commanded by a single unity of conception. And we think—though I cannot tell—that painting a great picture must require an intellect on the grand scale. There must be that all-embracing view which presents the beginning and the end, the whole and each part, as one instantaneous impression retentively and untiringly held in the mind. When we look at the larger Turners—canvases yards wide and tall—and observe that they are all done in one piece and represent one single second of time, and that every innumerable detail, however small, however distant, how-ever subordinate, is set forth naturally and in its true pro-portion and relation, without effort, without failure, we must feel in the presence of an intellectual manifestation the equal in quality and intensity of the finest achievements of warlike action, of forensic argument, or of scientific or philosophical adjudication.

In all battles two things are usually required of the Commander-in-Chief: to make a good plan for his army and, secondly, to keep a strong reserve. Both these are also obligatory upon the painter. To make a plan, thorough reconnaissance of the country where the battle is to be fought is needed. Its fields, its mountains, its rivers, its bridges, its trees, its flowers, its atmosphere—all require and repay attentive observation from a special point of view. One is quite astonished to find how many things there are in the landscape, and in every object in it, one never noticed before. And, this is a tremendous new pleasure and interest which invests every walk or drive with an added object. So many colours on the hillside, each different in shadow and in sunlight; such brilliant reflections in the pool, each a key lower than what they repeat; such lovely lights gilding or silvering surface or outline, all tinted exquisitely with pale colour, rose, orange, green, or violet. I found myself instinctively as I walked noting the tint and character of a leaf, the dreamy, purple shades of mountains, the exquisite lacery of winter branches, the dim, pale silhouettes of far horizons. And I had lived for over forty years without ever noticing any of them except in a general way, as one might look at a crowd and say, 'What a lot of people!'

I think this heightened sense of observation of Nature is one of the chief delights that have come to me through trying to paint. No doubt many people who are lovers of

art have acquired it in a high degree without actually practising. But I expect that nothing will make one observe
more quickly or more thoroughly than having to face the
difficulty of representing the thing observed. And mind
you, if you do observe accurately and with refinement,
and if you do record what you have seen with tolerable
correspondence, the result follows on the canvas with
startling obedience. Even if only four or five main
features are seized and truly recorded, these by themselves
will carry a lot of ill-success or half-success. Answer five
big questions out of all the hundreds in the examination
paper correctly and well, and though you may not win a
prize, at any rate you will not be absolutely ploughed.

But in order to make his plan, the General must not
only reconnoitre the battle-ground, he must also study the
achievements of the great Captains of the past. He must
bring the observations he has collected in the field into
comparison with the treatment of similar incidents by
famous chiefs. Then the galleries of Europe take on a new
—and to me at least a severely practical—interest. 'This,
then, is how ——— painted a cataract. Exactly, and there is
that same light I noticed last week in the waterfall at ———.'
And so on. You see the difficulty that baffled you yester-
day; and you see how easily it has been overcome by a
great or even by a skilful painter. Not only is your observation of Nature sensibly improved and developed, but
you look at the masterpieces of art with an analysing and
a comprehending eye.

The whole world is open with all its treasures. The
simplest objects have their beauty. Every garden presents

innumerable fascinating problems. Every land, every parish, has its own tale to tell. And there are many lands differing from each other in countless ways, and each presenting delicious variants of colour, light, form, and definition. Obviously, then, armed with a paint-box, one cannot be bored, one cannot be left at a loose end, one cannot 'have several days on one's hands.' Good gracious! what there is to admire and how little time there is to see it in! For the first time one begins to envy Methuselah. No doubt he made a very indifferent use of his opportunities.

But it is in the use and withholding of their reserves that the great Commanders have generally excelled. After all, when once the last reserve has been thrown in, the Commander's part is played. If that does not win the battle, he has nothing else to give. The event must be left to luck and to the fighting troops. But these last, in the absence of high direction, are apt to get into sad confusion, all mixed together in a nasty mess, without order or plan—and consequently without effect. Mere masses count no more. The largest brush, the brightest colours, cannot even make an impression. The pictorial battlefield becomes a sea of mud mercifully veiled by the fog of war. It is evident there has been a serious defeat. Even though the General plunges in himself and emerges bespattered, as he sometimes does, he will not retrieve the day.

In painting, the reserves consist in Proportion or Relation. And it is here that the art of the painter marches along the road which is traversed by all the greatest harmonies in thought. At one side of the palette there is white, at the other black; and neither is ever used 'neat.'

Between these two rigid limits all the action must lie, all the power required must be generated. Black and white themselves, placed in juxtaposition, make no great impression; and yet they are the most that you can do in pure contrast. It is wonderful—after one has tried and failed often—to see how easily and surely the true artist is able to produce every effect of light and shade, of sunshine and shadow, of distance or nearness, simply by expressing justly the relations between the different planes and surfaces with which he is dealing. We think that this is founded upon a sense of proportion, trained no doubt by practice, but which in its essence is a frigid manifestation of mental power and size. We think that the same mind's eye that can justly survey and appraise and prescribe beforehand the values of a truly great picture in one all-embracing regard, in one flash of simultaneous and homogeneous comprehension, would also with a certain acquaintance with the special technique be able to pronounce with sureness upon any other high activity of the human intellect. This was certainly true of the great Italians.

I have written in this way to show how varied are the delights which may be gained by those who enter hopefully and thoughtfully upon the pathway of painting; how enriched they will be in their daily vision, how fortified in their independence, how happy in their leisure. Whether you feel that your soul is pleased by the conception or contemplation of harmonies, or that your mind is stimulated by the aspect of magnificent problems, or whether you are content to find fun in trying to observe and depict the jolly things you see, the vistas of possibility are limited only by the shortness of life. Every day you may make progress. Every step may be fruitful. Yet there will stretch out before you an ever-lengthening, ever-ascending, ever-improving path. You know you will never get to the end of the journey. But this, so far from discouraging, only adds to the joy and glory of the climb.

Try it, then, before it is too late and before you mock at me. Try it while there is time to overcome the preliminary difficulties. Learn enough of the language in your prime to open this new literature to your age. Plant a garden in which you can sit when digging days are done. It may be only a small garden, but you will see it grow. Year by year it will bloom and ripen. Year by year it will be better cultivated. The weeds will be cast out. The fruit-trees will be pruned and trained. The flowers will bloom in more beautiful combinations. There will be sunshine there even in the winter-time, and cool shade, and the play of shadow on the pathway in the shining days of June.

I must say I like bright colours. I agree with Ruskin in his denunciation of that school of painting who 'eat slate-pencil and chalk, and assure everybody that they are nicer and purer than strawberries and plums.' I cannot pretend to feel impartial about the colours. I rejoice with the brilliant ones, and am genuinely sorry for the poor browns. When I get to heaven I mean to spend a considerable portion of my first million years in painting, and so get to the bottom of the subject. But then I shall require a still gayer palette than I get here below. I expect orange and vermilion will be the darkest, dullest colours upon it, and beyond them there will be a whole range of wonderful new colours which will delight the celestial eye.

Chance led me one autumn to a secluded nook on the Côte d'Azur, between Marseilles and Toulon, and there I fell in with one or two painters who revelled in the methods of the modern French school. These were disciples of Cézanne. They view Nature as a mass of shimmering light in which forms and surfaces are comparatively unimportant, indeed hardly visible, but which gleams and glows with beautiful harmonies and contrasts of colour. Certainly it was of great interest to me to come suddenly in contact with this entirely different way of looking at things. I had hitherto painted the sea flat, with long, smooth strokes of mixed pigment in which the tints varied only by gradations. Now I must try to represent it by innumerable small separate lozenge-shaped points and patches of colour—often pure colour—so that it looked more like a tessellated pavement than a marine picture. It sounds curious. All the same, do not be in a hurry to reject the method. Go back a few yards and survey the result. Each of these little points of colour is now playing his part in the general effect. Individually invisible, he sets up a strong radiation, of which the eye is conscious without detecting the cause. Look also at the blue of the Mediterranean. How can you depict and record it? Certainly not by any single colour that was ever manufactured. The only way in which that luminous intensity of blue can be simulated is by this multitude of tiny points of varied colour all in true relation to the rest of the scheme. Difficult? Fascinating!

Nature presents itself to the eye through the agency of these individual points of light, each of which sets up the vibrations peculiar to its colour. The brilliancy of a picture must therefore depend partly upon the frequency with which these points are found on any given area of the canvas, and partly on their just relation to one another. Ruskin says in his *Elements of Drawing*, from which I have already quoted, 'You will not, in Turner's largest oil pictures, perhaps six or seven feet long by four or five high, find one spot of colour as large as a grain of wheat ungradated.' But the gradations of Turner differ from those of the modern French school by being gently and almost imperceptibly evolved one from another instead of being bodily and even roughly separated; and the brush of Turner followed the form of the objects he depicted, while our French friends often seem to take a pride in directly opposing it. For instance, they would prefer to paint a sea with up and down strokes rather than with horizontal; or a tree-trunk from right to left rather than up and down. This, I expect, is due to falling in love with one's theories, and making sacrifices of truth to them in order to demonstrate fidelity and admiration.

But surely we owe a debt to those who have so wonderfully vivified, brightened, and illuminated modern landscape painting. Have not Manet and Monet, Cézanne and Matisse, rendered to painting something of the same service which Keats and Shelley gave to poetry after the solemn and ceremonious literary perfections of the eighteenth century? They have brought back to the pictorial art a new draught of *joie de vivre*; and the beauty of their work is instinct with gaiety, and floats in sparkling air.

I do not expect these masters would particularly appreciate my defence, but I must avow an increasing attraction to their work. Lucid and exact expression is one of the characteristics of the French mind. The French language has been made the instrument of the admirable gift. Frenchmen talk and write just as well about painting as they have done about love, about war, about diplomacy, or cooking. Their terminology is precise and complete. They are therefore admirably equipped to be teachers in the theory of any of these arts. Their critical faculty is so powerfully developed that it is perhaps some restraint upon achievement. But it is a wonderful corrective to others as well as to themselves.

My French friend, for instance, after looking at some of my daubs, took me round the galleries of Paris, pausing here and there. Wherever he paused, I found myself before a picture which I particularly admired. He then explained that it was quite easy to tell, from the kind of things I had been trying to do, what were the things I liked. Never having taken any interest in pictures till I tried to paint, I had no preconceived opinions. I just felt, for reasons I could not fathom, that I liked some much more than others. I was astonished that anyone else should, on the most cursory observation of my work, be able so surely to divine a taste which I had never consciously formed. My friend said that it is not a bad thing to know nothing at all about pictures, but to have a matured mind trained in other things and a new strong interest for painting. The elements are there from which a true taste in art can be formed with time and guidance, and there are no obstacles or imperfect conceptions in the way. I hope this is true. Certainly the last part is true.

Once you begin to study it, all Nature is equally interesting and equally charged with beauty. I was shown a picture by Cézanne of a blank wall of a house, which he had made instinct with the most delicate lights and colours. Now I often amuse myself when I am looking at a wall or a flat surface of any kind by trying to distinguish all the different colours and tints which can be discerned upon it, and considering whether these arise from reflections or from natural hue. You would be astonished the first time you tried this to see how many and what beautiful colours there are even in the most commonplace objects, and the more carefully and frequently you look the more variations do you perceive.

But these are no reasons for limiting oneself to the plainest and most ordinary objects and scenes. Mere prettiness of scene, to be sure, is not needed for a beautiful picture. In fact, artificially-made pretty places are very often a hindrance to a good picture. Nature will hardly stand a double process of beautification: one layer of idealism on top of another is too much of a good thing. But a vivid scene, a brilliant atmosphere, novel and charming lights, impressive contrasts, if they strike the eye all at once, arouse an interest and an ardour which will certainly be reflected in the work which you try to do, and will make it seem easier.

It would be interesting if some real authority investigated carefully the part which memory plays in painting.

We look at the object with an intent regard, then at the palette, and thirdly at the canvas. The canvas receives a message dispatched usually a few seconds before from the natural object. But it has come through a post-office *en route*. It has been transmitted in code. It has been turned from light into paint. It reaches the canvas a cryptogram. Not until it has been placed in its correct relation to everything else that is on the canvas can it be deciphered, is its meaning apparent, is it translated once again from mere pigment into light. And the light this time is not of Nature but of Art. The whole of this considerable process is carried through on the wings or the wheels of memory. In most cases we think it is the wings—airy and quick like a butterfly from flower to flower. But all heavy traffic and all that has to go a long journey must travel on wheels.

In painting in the open air the sequence of actions is so rapid that the process of translation into and out of pigment may seem to be unconscious. But all the greatest landscapes have been painted indoors, and often long after the first impressions were gathered. In a dim cellar the Dutch or Italian master recreated the gleaming ice of a Netherlands carnival or the lustrous sunshine of Venice or the Campagna. Here, then, is required a formidable memory of the visual kind. Not only do we develop our powers of observation, but also those of carrying the record—of carrying it through an extraneous medium and of reproducing it, hours, days, or even months after the scene has vanished or the sunlight died.

I was told by a friend that when Whistler guided a school in Paris he made his pupils observe their model on the ground floor, and then run upstairs and paint their picture piece by piece on the floor above. As they became more proficient, he put their easels up a storey higher, till at last the *élite* were scampering with their decision up six flights into the attic—praying it would not evaporate on the way. This is, perhaps, only a tale. But it shows effectively of what enormous importance a trained, accurate, retentive memory must be to an artist; and conversely what a useful exercise painting may be for the development of an accurate and retentive memory.

There is no better exercise for the would-be artist than to study and devour a picture, and then, without looking at it again, to attempt the next day to reproduce it. Nothing can more exactly measure the progress both of observation and memory. It is still harder to compose out of many separate, well-retained impressions, aided though they be by sketches and colour notes, a new, complete conception. But this is the only way in which great landscapes have been painted—or can be painted. The size of the canvas alone precludes its being handled out of doors. The fleeting light imposes a rigid time-limit. The same light never returns. One cannot go back day after day without the picture getting stale. The painter must choose between a rapid impression, fresh and warm and living, but probably deserving only of a short life, and the cold, profound, intense effort of memory, knowledge, and will-power, prolonged perhaps for weeks, from which a masterpiece can alone result. It is much better not to fret too much about the latter. Leave to the masters of art trained by a lifetime of devotion the wonderful process of picture-building and picture-creation. Go out into the sunlight and be happy with what you see.

Painting is complete as a distraction. I know of nothing which, without exhausting the body, more entirely absorbs the mind. Whatever the worries of the hour or the threats of the future, once the picture has begun to flow along, there is no room for them in the mental screen. They pass out into shadow and darkness. All one's mental light, such as it is, becomes concentrated on the task. Time stands respectfully aside, and it is only after many hesitations that luncheon knocks gruffly at the door. When I have had to stand up on parade, or even, I regret to say, in church, for half an hour at a time, I have always felt that the erect position is not natural to man, has only been painfully acquired, and is only with fatigue and difficulty maintained. But no one who is fond of painting finds the slightest inconvenience, as long as the interest holds, in standing to paint for three or four hours at a stretch.

Lastly, let me say a word on painting as a spur to travel. There is really nothing like it. Every day and all day is provided with its expedition and its occupation—cheap, attainable, innocent, absorbing, recuperative. The vain racket of the tourist gives place to the calm enjoyment of the philosopher, intensified by an enthralling sense of action and endeavour. Every country where the sun shines and every district in it, has a theme of its own. The lights, the atmosphere, the aspect, the spirit, are all different ; but each has its native charm. Even if you are only a poor painter you can feel the influence of the scene, guiding your brush, selecting the tubes you squeeze on to the palette. Even if you cannot portray it as you see it, you feel it, you know it, and you admire it for ever. When people rush about Europe in the train from one glittering centre of work or pleasure to another, passing—at enormous expense—through a series of mammoth hotels and blatant carnivals, they little know what they are missing, and how cheaply priceless things can be obtained. The painter wanders and loiters contentedly from place to place, always on the look out for some brilliant butterfly of a picture which can be caught and set up and carried safely home.

Now I am learning to like painting even on dull days. But in my hot youth I demanded sunshine. Sir William Orpen advised me to visit Avignon on account of its wonderful light, and certainly there is no more delightful centre for a would-be painter's activities: then Egypt, fierce and brilliant, presenting in infinite variety the single triplex theme of the Nile, the desert, and the sun; or Palestine, a land of rare beauty—the beauty of the turquoise and the opal—which well deserves the attention of some real artist, and has never been portrayed to the extent that is its due. And what of India? Who has ever interpreted its lurid splendours? But after all, if only the sun will shine, one does not need to go beyond one's own country. There is nothing more intense than the burnished steel and gold of a Highland stream; and at the beginning and close of almost every day the Thames displays to the citizens of London glories and delights which one must travel far to rival.

SOME PAINTINGS

BY

The Right Honourable

SIR WINSTON CHURCHILL

K.G., O.M., C.H., M.P.

1. A Vase of Flowers

2. *The Loup River, Quebec. Exhibited
at the Royal Academy, 1947*

4. *The Tapestries at Blenheim Palace.*
Exhibited at the Royal Academy, 1948

5. *The Blue Room, Trent Park, the home of the late Sir Philip Sassoon. Exhibited at the Royal Academy, 1948*

6. Village near Lugano, September, 1945

7. *Olive grove, La Dragonière, near Monte Carlo*

8. Church by Lake Como, September, 1945

9. *The Goldfish Pool at Chartwell, in the
garden of Mr. Churchill's Kent home.
Exhibited at the Royal Academy, 1948*

10. *The Weald of Kent under Snow, painted from Chartwell*

11. Orchids

12. *The Mill, Saint-Georges-Motel,*
    Normandy

14. *The Mediterranean near Genoa,*
September, 1945

15. St. Jean, Cap Ferrat

17. By Lake Lugano, 1945

*18. Chartwell under Snow. Exhibited at
the Royal Academy, 1947*